Hamsters

by Helen Frost

Consulting Editor: Gail Saunders-Smith, Ph.D.

Consultant: Jennifer Zablotny, D.V.M.,
Member, American Animal Hospital Association

Pebble Books

an imprint of Capstone Press
Mankato, Minnesota

Pebble Books are published by Capstone Press
151 Good Counsel Drive, P.O. Box 669, Mankato, Minnesota 56002
http://www.capstone-press.com

2 3 4 5 6 06 05 04 03 02

Library of Congress Cataloging-in-Publication Data
Frost, Helen, 1949–
  Hamsters/by Helen Frost.
    p. cm.—(All about pets)
  Includes bibliographical references and index.
  Summary: Simple text and photographs present the features and care of
hamsters.
  ISBN 0-7368-0658-X
  1. Hamsters as pets—Juvenile literature. [1. Hamsters. 2. Pets.] I. Title. II. All
about pets (Mankato, Minn.)
SF459.H3 F76 2001
636.9'356—dc21

00-022986

Note to Parents and Teachers

The All About Pets series supports national science standards for units on the diversity and unity of life. This book describes hamsters and illustrates what they need from their owners. The photographs support emergent readers in understanding the text. The repetition of words and phrases helps emergent readers learn new words. This book also introduces emergent readers to subject-specific vocabulary words, which are defined in the Words to Know section. Emergent readers may need assistance to read some words and to use the Table of Contents, Words to Know, Read More, Internet Sites, and Index/Word List sections of the book.

Table of Contents

Hamsters are pets.

Hamsters have fur.

8

Hamsters have
cheek pouches.

Hamsters sleep
during the day.

Hamsters play
during the night.

Hamsters need
a clean cage.

Hamsters need bedding.

Hamsters need
food and water.

20

Hamsters need
a place to exercise.

Words to Know

bedding—something used to make a bed; hamsters use wood shavings, hay, and shredded paper for bedding.

cage—a container in which an animal is kept; a hamster needs clean bedding in its cage.

cheek pouch—a pocket of skin in the side of some animals' mouths; hamsters carry food in their cheek pouches.

exercise—to be active; hamsters run and play to exercise; they sometimes run on an exercise wheel.

fur—the soft, thick, hairy coat of an animal; the fur of hamsters can be white, gray, black, or brown.

pet—a tame animal kept for company or pleasure

Read More

Engfer, LeeAnne. *My Pet Hamster and Gerbils.* All About Pets. Minneapolis: Lerner Publications, 1997.

Evans, Mark. *Hamster.* ASPCA Pet Care Guides for Kids. New York: Dorling Kindersley, 1993.

Meredith, Susan. *Hamsters.* Usborne First Pets. London: Usborne, 1999.

Vrbova, Zuza. *Hamsters.* Junior Pet Care. Philadelphia: Chelsea House, 1997.

Internet Sites

Critter Collection: Hamsters as Pets
http://animalnetwork.com/critters/profiles/
hamster/default.asp

Hamsterific.com: Hamster Care!
http://www.hamsterific.com/hamstercare.asp

Hamsters
http://www.petwebsite.com/hamsters.htm

Index/Word List

are, 5
bedding, 17
cage, 15
cheek, 9
clean, 15
day, 11
during, 11, 13
exercise, 21
food, 19
fur, 7

have, 7, 9
need, 15, 17, 19, 21
night, 13
pets, 5
place, 21
play, 13
pouches, 9
sleep, 11
water, 19

Word Count: 39
Early-Intervention Level: 5

Editorial Credits
Martha E. H. Rustad, editor; Linda Clavel, designer; Jodi Theisen and Katy Kudela,
  photo researchers; Crystal Graf, photo editor

Photo Credits
David F. Clobes, 10, 12, 14
Eyewire, cover
Joan Balzarini, 1, 6, 18
Norvia Behling, 8, 16, 20
Unicorn Stock Photos/Tommy Dodson, 4

The author thanks the children's section staff at the Allen County Public Library in
Fort Wayne, Indiana, for research assistance. The author also thanks Nancy T.
Whitesell, D.V.M., at St. Joseph Animal Hospital in Fort Wayne, Indiana.